Presented to

Mack Phillips

From

Shannon Groth

On this date

12 · 7 · 07

Find Your *Wings*

Mark Harris
with Karen Moore

HOWARD BOOKS
A DIVISION OF SIMON & SCHUSTER
New York   London   Toronto   Sydney

Our purpose at Howard Books is to:

➤ *Increase faith* in the hearts of growing Christians
➤ *Inspire holiness* in the lives of believers
➤ *Instill hope* in the hearts of struggling people everywhere

Because He's coming again!

HOWARD

Published by Howard Books, a division of Simon & Schuster, Inc.
1230 Avenue of the Americas, New York, NY 10020

Find Your Wings © 2006 by Howard Books

The Song "Find Your Wings" written by Mark Harris and Tony Wood
2005 RyanLynn Publishing (adm by New Spring, a division of Zomba Enterprises, Inc.)/ASCAP, New Spring, a division of Zomba Enterprises, Inc./ASCAP, Row J, Seat 9 (adm by New Spring, a division of Zomba Enterprises, Inc)/ASCAP

10 Digit ISBN: 1-58229-677-4. 13 Digit ISBN: 978-1-58229-667-7
10 Digit ISBN: 1-4165-3759-7. 13 Digit ISBN: 978-1-4165-3759-5

10 9   8 7 6 5 4 3 2 1

HOWARD is a registered trademark of Simon & Schuster, Inc.

Manufactured in the United States.

For information regarding special discounts for bulk purchases, please contact Simon & Schuster Special Sales at 1-800-456-6798 or business@simonandschuster.com.

Edited by Chrys Howard
Cover and interior design by Left Coast Design, Portland, OR 97219

This book is dedicated to my parents, Harry and Doris Harris, who helped me find my wings, and to my children, Matthew and Maddison, who give me joy while I help them find their wings.

If I ride the wings of the morning,

if I dwell by the farthest oceans,

even there your hand will guide me,

and your strength will support me.

PSALM 139:9–10 NLT

Introduction

Your personal journey begins with the very first "yes." It is your response to a call that emanates so close to the heart, you need silence to even hear it beckon. It is the step that leads you past the comfort of what you've always been and always known to the place you're meant to be.

Some of you begin searching for the path before you've even reached the maturity to leave your mother's protective wing. Some of you don't begin until an unexpected, sacred moment confronts your darkness and awakens you to light.

Once the journey has begun, the call grows louder, the pace gets faster, and the desire to soar becomes a precious reality. That is the point when you release the hand of those behind you and embrace all that is ahead. It is the moment when you detect the first flutter, the moment you begin to "find your wings."

It's only for a moment
you are mine to hold . . .

CHAPTER 1

Live for Today

Ask any mother about the moment when she first held her newborn, and she'll tell you it was one of the best moments of her life—but it passed too quickly. She'll hold that moment forever in her heart though.

Try as we might, we can't control time. It insists on having its way and hardly nods at us as it goes right out of our control. Another candle lights up a birthday cake, another moment is created and enjoyed, time marches on, and the next moment appears.

The best way to stop time in its tracks is to make it a friend. Enjoy the moments you've been blessed with. Hold each one as a precious gift. Record it in your journal, give God thanks for it, and honor the gift of now.

Remember the saying. . .

Look to this day. . . for yesterday is but a dream,
And tomorrow is only a vision. . .
But today well-lived
makes every yesterday a dream of happiness
and every tomorrow a vision of hope.

Know the true value of time; snatch,

seize, and enjoy every moment of

it. No idleness, no laziness,

no procrastination.

LORD CHESTERFIELD

You'll find as you grow older

that you weren't born such a

very great while ago after all.

The time shortens up.

WILLIAM DEAN HOWELLS

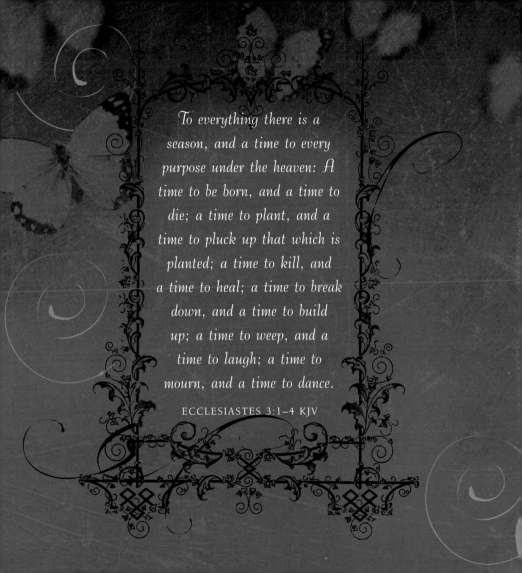

To everything there is a season, and a time to every purpose under the heaven: A time to be born, and a time to die; a time to plant, and a time to pluck up that which is planted; a time to kill, and a time to heal; a time to break down, and a time to build up; a time to weep, and a time to laugh; a time to mourn, and a time to dance.

ECCLESIASTES 3:1–4 KJV

The plans that heaven has for you
will all too soon unfold . . .

CHAPTER 2

Welcome Tomorrow

Ah, here's the blessing in letting time pass. Heaven's plans have an opportunity to unfold. You have a chance to become all that God meant for you to become. He isn't quickly sketching up something in case you move on. He has already designed everything for your good, and if you don't move forward, you may not get to discover the prosperity and joy intended just for you. This is your time to be enriched by His grace and love, because He's already planned it all and has gone on ahead of you. He's waiting to share incredible hope and a bright future.

That's an intriguing invitation, a fabulous reason to keep moving. Let this be your season to grow and change. Time will not stand still, but neither will you, and you will not want to. The future is too exciting to let it pass you by!

I learned that one can never go back,

that one should not ever try to go back—

that the essence of life is going forward.

Life is really a one-way street, isn't it?

AGATHA CHRISTIE

I'll Give You Wings to Fly

Walk with me along the path
And reach up toward the sky,
I'll be right there beside you
Through each new thing you try.
And any time you're ready
I'll give you wings to fly.

If you come upon some roadblocks
That you struggle to get through,
Just know that I have gone ahead,
To clear the path for you.
And soon you'll find the place
That you've been walking to.

Walk with me; talk with me.
I'll hear each laugh and cry.
I'll be your help in trouble,
Your protector and ally.
And any time you're ready
I'll give you wings to fly.

KAREN MOORE

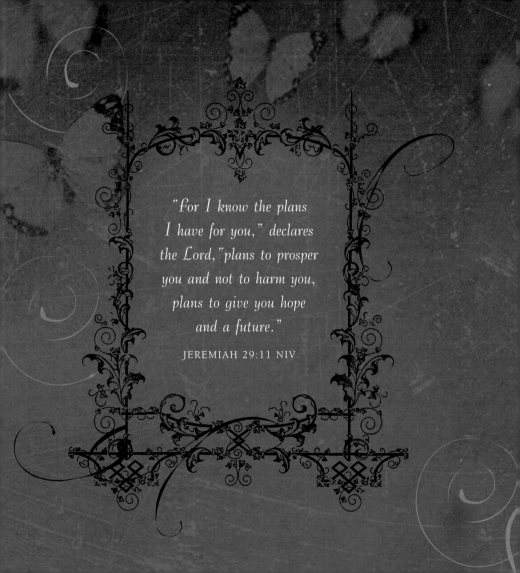

"For I know the plans
I have for you," declares
the Lord, "plans to prosper
you and not to harm you,
plans to give you hope
and a future."

JEREMIAH 29:11 NIV

So many different
prayers I'll pray
for all that
you might do.
But most of all
I'll want to know
you're walking in
the truth . . .

CHAPTER 3

Pray Daily

Matthew Henry said that "when God is about to give His People the expected good, He pours out a Spirit of prayer, and it is a good sign that He is coming towards them in mercy."

With each step of your journey and each prayer spoken on your behalf, you are drawn closer to the One who planned good things for you.

How does prayer help you along the path? Why is it essential to finding your wings? Augustine of Hippo reminded us that "prayer is not merely expressing our present desires. Its purpose is to exercise and train our desires so that we want what he is getting ready to give us. His gift is very great, and we are small vessels for receiving it. So prayer involves widening our hearts to God."

Never doubt the power of prayer. Never doubt God's love for you and His desire that you have a future rich in blessings. Ask and you shall receive, knock and the door will be opened.

God has the same desire that others who love you have for you. God wants you to walk in the ways of truth. The world will try to distract you, delay you, and create obstacles to your path of truth. The world will try to hide your wings. Prayer will strengthen and renew you and guide you into all truth.

KAREN MOORE

Take Time to Pray

I got up early one morning
And rushed right into the day;
I had so much to accomplish
That I didn't take time to pray.

Problems just tumbled about me,
And heavier came each task;
"Why doesn't God help me?" I wondered.
He answered, "You didn't ask."

I wanted to see joy and beauty,
But the day toiled on gray and bleak;
I wondered why God didn't show me.
He said, "But you didn't seek."

I tried to come into God's presence;
I used all my keys in the lock.
God gently and lovingly chided,
"My child, you didn't knock."

I woke up early this morning,
And paused before entering the day;
I had so much to accomplish
That I had to take time to pray.

AUTHOR UNKNOWN

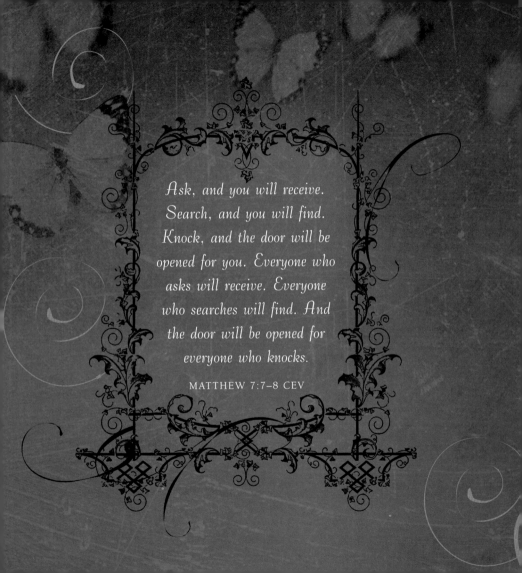

Ask, and you will receive.
Search, and you will find.
Knock, and the door will be
opened for you. Everyone who
asks will receive. Everyone
who searches will find. And
the door will be opened for
everyone who knocks.

MATTHEW 7:7–8 CEV

May passion be the wind
that leads you through your days . . .

CHAPTER 4

Choose Passionately

Life offers you many choices. It blesses you with options about how to spend your time, your energy, and your very existence. It encourages your dreams, promises you a future, and announces itself at every turn. At some point your wings will be all aflutter as life shows you a path that hits the very center of your being, the place where passion is born. That's the place of connection where your dreams and God's plans for your life connect. What will you choose?

Phillips Brooks said this about life: "The great danger facing all of us is not that we shall make an absolute failure of life, not that we shall fall into outright viciousness, nor that we shall be terribly unhappy, nor that we shall feel that life has no meaning at all—not these things. The danger is that we may fail to perceive life's greatest meaning, fall short of its highest good, miss its deepest and most abiding happiness, be unable to tender the most needed service, be unconscious of life ablaze with the light of the Presence of God—and be content to have it so."

In other words, are we willing to get past the comfortable, the okay, the expected path of life, and go for the passion that God meant for us to enjoy? Life offers many choices. Find the wings of passion and ride them on the winds of joy. Only there can you experience the abundant life!

We may affirm absolutely that nothing great in the world has ever been accomplished without passion.

GEORG HEGEL

Do not follow where the path may lead. Go instead where there is no path and leave a trail.

RALPH WALDO EMERSON

Whatever you do, work at
it with all your heart, as
working for the Lord.

COLOSSIANS 3:23 NIV

And may
conviction keep
you strong, guide
you on your way.

CHAPTER 5

Know Yourself

Hello, who are you? How do you define yourself? Are you your family? That is, you were born into the Smith family, so are you a Smith? Are you what you do for a living? Are you what you eat?

To consider the idea "to thine own self be true," you have to be able to identify just who you are. Thomas à Kempis said, "A humble knowledge of yourself is a surer way to God than a deep search after learning." In other words, the more you understand the person God created you to be, the more you'll understand God Himself. That alone makes it a worthwhile journey.

The seed of truth was planted in your heart long ago, and as you grow and truth takes root within you, it will give you wings. That is who you are: the keeper of a God-given truth and an example of that truth in the world.

All Christians are called to unity

in love and unity in truth.

AUTHOR UNKNOWN

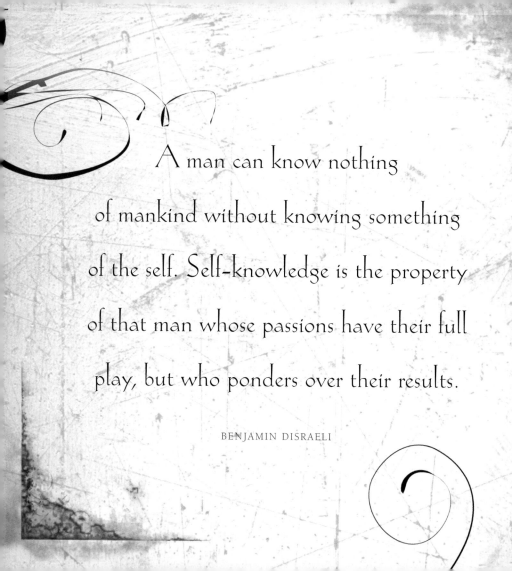

A man can know nothing

of mankind without knowing something

of the self. Self-knowledge is the property

of that man whose passions have their full

play, but who ponders over their results.

BENJAMIN DISRAELI

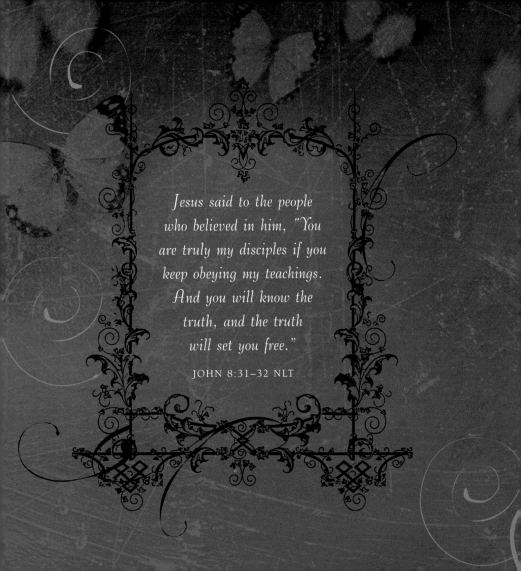

Jesus said to the people
who believed in him, "You
are truly my disciples if you
keep obeying my teachings.
And you will know the
truth, and the truth
will set you free."

JOHN 8:31–32 NLT

May there be many moments
that make your life so sweet . . .

CHAPTER 6

Include God

What if the future were all up to you? Think about it. You could add anything to it you wanted and take away things you didn't want. It would be the world according to you. Imagine! It would be like you totally had free will.

Hold on! You do have free will. God gave you that when you were born. He allowed you to think for yourself, make your own choices, go where you want to go, and do what you want to do. Maybe that's why we're not always so confident about the future.

We have a lot of say about what happens to us, and honestly, that means we have no one to blame but ourselves.

Here's a better plan. Designing your future works better when you let God in on the direction you hope to go. The more you include His will with your will, the better the future will feel. You don't really want to go it alone in the world, anyway. It's good to know that someone has already gone ahead of you and knows just where you're going.

Eleanor Roosevelt said, "The future belongs to those who believe in the beauty of their dreams." If you've put your dreams in God's hand and asked His help in getting where you want to go, then the future is yours. Together you can create anything!

Far away there in the sunshine are my highest aspirations. I may not reach them, but I can look up and see their beauty, believe in them, and try to follow where they lead.

LOUISA MAY ALCOTT

First build a proper goal.

That proper goal will make

it easy, almost automatic,

to build a proper you.

JOHANN WOLFGANG VON GOETHE

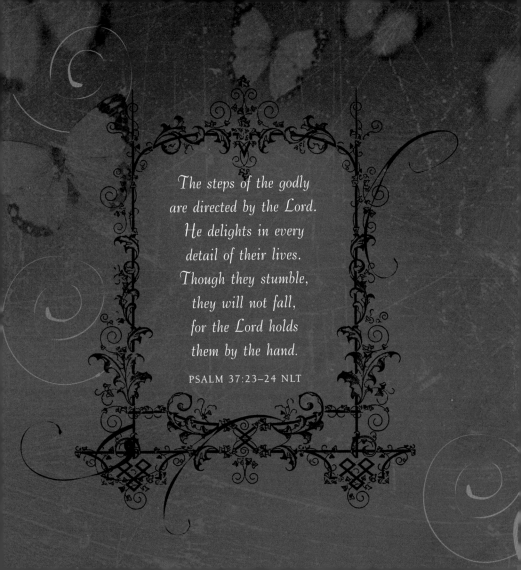

The steps of the godly
are directed by the Lord.
He delights in every
detail of their lives.
Though they stumble,
they will not fall,
for the Lord holds
them by the hand.

PSALM 37:23–24 NLT

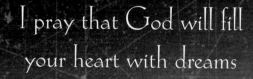

I pray that God will fill
your heart with dreams

And that faith gives you the courage
to dare to do great things . . .

CHAPTER 7

Dream Big

William Salter said, "As the essence of courage is to stake one's life on a possibility, so the essence of faith is to believe that the possibility exists."

Whatever you want to do in life will require you to be a "possibility" thinker! That means you not only seek your path with courage but that you believe it is totally possible for you to get where you want to go.

Courage walks hand in hand with fear. For most of us, whether we're attempting to set new goals or try a new sport or go on a first date, the event itself takes a certain amount of courage. Why? Because we always have some fear that we might fail. The question, "What great thing would you attempt to do if you knew with God's help you could not fail?" is worth pondering. It is the very essence of what courage is all about.

When you dare to attempt great things, you must keep your eye on the goal, for only then will you be sure to hit the mark. Courage looks at what you really believe. If you believe you will not win, the chances are good that you will not win. If you believe you are following God's plan for your life and therefore believe you will win, then winning is a much bigger possibility.

Martin Luther King, Jr., said that "courage breeds creative self-affirmation." In other words, you must think and say the things that will help you succeed. Have faith in yourself. Have faith in God. Have faith in the convictions of your dreams.

Courage is the best gift of all;

courage stands before everything. It is

what preserves our liberty, safety, life, and

our homes and parents, our country and our

children. Courage comprises all things: a

person with courage has every blessing.

PLAUTUS

Doubt sees the obstacles,

Faith sees the way;

Doubt sees the blackest night,

Faith sees the day.

Doubt dreads to take a step,

Faith soars on high;

Doubt questions, "Who believes?"

Faith answers, "I!"

AUTHOR UNKNOWN

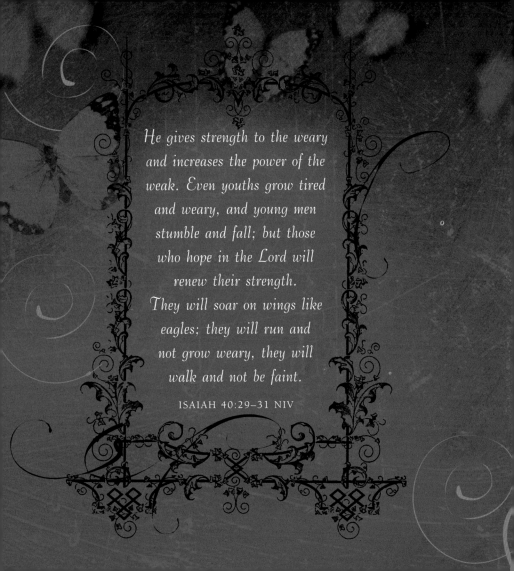

He gives strength to the weary
and increases the power of the
weak. Even youths grow tired
and weary, and young men
stumble and fall; but those
who hope in the Lord will
renew their strength.
They will soar on wings like
eagles; they will run and
not grow weary, they will
walk and not be faint.

ISAIAH 40:29–31 NIV

I'm here for you
whatever this
life brings,

So let my love
give you roots
and help you
find your wings.

CHAPTER 8

Cherish Your Roots

It was Hodding Carter, Jr., who said, "There are two lasting bequests we can give our children: One is roots. The other is wings."

When you were born into your family, you received a rich heritage from those who would become your cornerstone and your foundation. These were the people who would teach you the rules of the family and, later, the rules of the church and of society. It was their task to train you so that you would be firmly rooted in faith and nurtured in love. You learned by example, and you learned by experience.

Families are a beautiful thing when they function as God intended. When there is the right mixture of toughness and tenderness, of structure and creativity, of laughter and sorrow, then your roots are positive and strong and you grow happily and well. In this kind of family, you are truly blessed.

Once your life's foundation is set, you begin to need more space and more opportunity to discover the path meant just for you. That fluttering from deep within you becomes much louder and much more demanding. You have new wings.

Your family gave you a peek at what justice and kindness and acceptance are all about. Now as you embrace your dreams, you will discover even greater meaning for such words. Flying doesn't mean you've given up your roots; it just means you have a place to return to whenever you can. Your family is always there for you. You're free to fly!

Children Learn What They Live

ADAPTED FROM DOROTHY LAW NOLTE

If a child lives with criticism, he believes in criticizing.

If a child lives with hostility, he believes in bullying others.

If a child lives with ridicule, he believes he is not lovable.

If a child lives with shame, he believes he is at fault.

If a child lives with tolerance, he believes in the rights of others.

If a child lives with encouragement, he believes he can try again.

If a child lives with praise, he believes in saying "thank you."

If a child lives with fairness, he believes in justice.

If a child lives with security, he believes the world is safe.

If a child lives with approval, he believes he is worthwhile.

If a child lives with acceptance and friendship, he believes in love.

If a child lives with parents who have faith, he believes in God.

One must know oneself.

If this does not serve to discover truth,

it at least serves as a rule of life

and there is nothing better.

BLAISE PASCAL

God sets the lonely
in families.

PSALM 68:6 NIV

It's not living
if you don't
reach for
the sky . . .

CHAPTER 9

Reach for the Sky

C. S. Lewis wrote, "Aim at heaven and you will get earth thrown in. Aim at earth and you will get neither."

You've been living awhile now and you've probably got a pretty good grasp of what it means to set goals and plan for the future. Setting a goal might be the easy part. Really reaching for it is a bit tougher. The funny part about most goals is that they are always just out of your grasp and make you stretch a bit to capture them. That's aiming at heaven.

God's been watching over you for some time, and it really makes Him smile when you include Him in your plans. If you don't remember to do that, He'll watch over you anyway, but He can show you some really great shortcuts, if you'll invite Him to guide you where you want to go. After all, you're pretty special to Him, and He wants to be sure you get where you're aiming to go.

Vance Havner said, "The vision must be followed by the venture. It is not enough to stare up the steps—we must step up the stairs."

Every step you take increases the power of your wings, and when you reach the top, you know you can fly. Reach for the sky!

The world stands aside to let

anyone pass who knows

where he is going.

DAVID STARR JORDAN

Set yourself earnestly to discover

what you are made to do, and then

give yourself passionately

to the doing of it.

MARTIN LUTHER KING, JR.

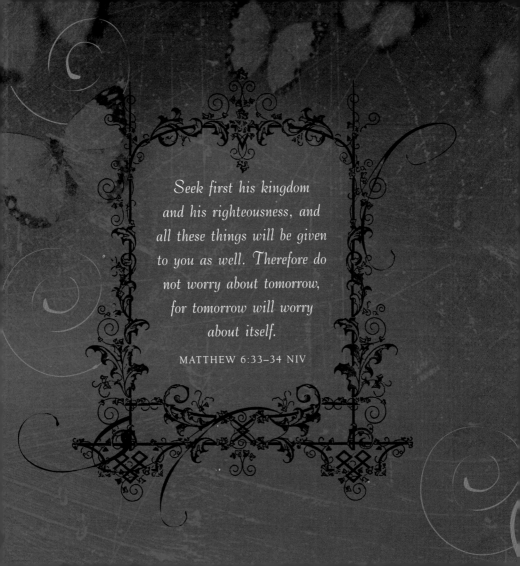

Seek first his kingdom
and his righteousness, and
all these things will be given
to you as well. Therefore do
not worry about tomorrow,
for tomorrow will worry
about itself.

MATTHEW 6:33–34 NIV

I'll have tears
as you take off,
but I'll cheer
as you fly!

CHAPTER 10

Go Ahead! Fly!

It's a proud moment. You've discovered your wings. You've set your course, and you're ready to take off. Those who love you are cheery and teary and so full of emotion, they hardly know what to say. Out of love for you, they want you to rise, to soar, to reach new heights meant just for you.

It's a thrilling moment. If you remember your first ride on an amazing roller coaster, it's something like that. At first you find yourself holding on tight, slowly taking off, ever so carefully going up up up! Just when you wonder if you can go any farther, you suddenly find yourself racing along, flying at full speed, hands in the air, and surrendering everything you've got to the experience. It's incredible! It's something you can hardly describe, but you know it's good, because it makes your blood pump faster and faster and your smile bigger and bigger.

The life coaster is going to be something like that. Sometimes you'll try new things and they'll never quite take you where you want to go. Another time your effort will launch you way beyond anything you had even dreamed was possible.

This is your moment. Embrace it. Tears of joy will send you off, and smiles of delight will welcome you back any time you're ready to come. Keep in mind that if you attempt great things for God, you can expect great things from God, for He will be with you every step of the way.

In your flight . . .

Be dogmatically true,

Obstinately holy,

Immovably honest.

Desperately kind,

Fixedly upright.

CHARLES HADDON SPURGEON

Find Your Wings

It's only for a moment you are mine to hold,

The plans that heaven has for you will all too soon unfold.

So many different prayers I'll pray for all that you might do.

But most of all I'll want to know you're walking in the truth.

And if I've never told you

I want you to know

As I watch you grow . . .

I pray that God will fill your heart with dreams

And that faith gives you the courage

To dare to do great things,

I'm here for you whatever this life brings,

So let my love give you roots

And help you find your wings.

May passion be the wind

That leads you through your days

And may conviction keep you strong,

Guide you on your way.

May there be many moments

That make your life so sweet

But more than memories . . .

It's not living if you don't reach for the sky,

I'll have tears as you take off,

But I'll cheer as you fly!

"*Everything is possible
for him who believes.*"

MARK 9:23 NIV